TRUMPET

BROADWAY & HOLLYWOOD *Classics*

TRUMPET

CONTENTS

ISBN 1-575-60495-7

Performance Disclaimer:
These arrangements are for personal performance use only. The use of costumes, choreography or other elements that evoke the story or characters of a legitimate stage musical work is prohibited in the absence of a performance license.

Visit our website at www.cherrylane.com

◆ WE GO TOGETHER

From GREASE

TRUMPET

Lyric and Music by WARREN CASEY
and JIM JACOBS

Bright fifties Rock

2 DAY-O
(The Banana Boat Song)
From BEETLEJUICE

Words and Music by IRVING BURGIE
and WILLIAM ATTAWAY

TRUMPET

❸ MY FAVORITE THINGS

From THE SOUND OF MUSIC

TRUMPET

Lyrics by OSCAR HAMMERSTEIN II
Music by RICHARD RODGERS

5

6

◆₄ SOMEDAY OUT OF THE BLUE
(Theme From El Dorado)
From THE ROAD TO EL DORADO

TRUMPET

Music by ELTON JOHN and PATRICK LEONARD
Lyrics by TIM RICE

❺ LEAVING ON A JET PLANE

From ARMAGEDDON

TRUMPET

Words and Music by
JOHN DENVER

8

8

6

8

❻ THE CANDY MAN
From WILLY WONKA AND THE CHOCOLATE FACTORY

TRUMPET

Words and Music by LESLIE BRICUSSE
and ANTHONY NEWLEY

◆7 THIS IS THE MOMENT

From JEKYLL & HYDE

TRUMPET

Words by LESLIE BRICUSSE
Music by FRANK WILDHORN

❽ CONSIDER YOURSELF

From the Columbia Pictures - Romulus Motion Picture Production of Lionel Bart's OLIVER!

TRUMPET

Words and Music by
LIONEL BART

◆ 9 (I'VE HAD) THE TIME OF MY LIFE

From DIRTY DANCING

TRUMPET

Words and Music by FRANKE PREVITE
JOHN DeNICOLA and DONALD MARKOWITZ

WHEN YOU BELIEVE

From THE PRINCE OF EGYPT

TRUMPET

Words and Music Composed by STEPHEN SCHWARTZ
with Additional Music by BABYFACE

THE ENTERTAINER

Featured in the Motion Picture THE STING

TRUMPET

SCOTT JOPLIN

Lower notes opt.

◆12 THE IMPOSSIBLE DREAM
(The Quest)
From MAN OF LA MANCHA

TRUMPET

Lyric by JOE DARION
Music by MITCH LEIGH